CW00542329

The God Who Says Sorry

By

Anthony Bird

The God Who Says Sorry
By
Anthony Bird

Copyright © 2010 by Anthony Bird in accordance with the Copyright, Designs and Patents Act 1998.

All rights reserved. No part of this publication may be reproduced, stored in a retrieval system or transmitted in any form or by any means electronic, mechanical, audio, visual or otherwise, without prior permission of the copyright owner. Nor can it be circulated in any form of binding or cover other than that in which it is published and without similar conditions including this condition being imposed on the subsequent purchaser.

ISBN: 978-0-9566597-0-5

Published by Anthony Bird in conjunction with Writersworld Ltd and is available to order from most book shops and internet book retailers throughout the United Kingdom

Edited by Brian Stanton

Cover Design by Charles Leveroni

Printed and bound by
www.printondemand-worldwide.com

www.writersworld.co.uk
Writersworld, 2 Bear Close Flats, Bear Close, Woodstock, Oxfordshire, OX20 1JX, United Kingdom

The text pages of this book are produced via an independent certification process that ensures the trees from which the paper is produced come from well managed sources that exclude the risk of using illegally logged timber while leaving options to use recycled paper as well.

This book is dedicated to

Tony Foottit,

Robin Morrell (died 11th March 2010),

Alex Wedderspoon,

and to the memory of Noel Whitehouse Bird.

ACKNOWLEDGMENTS

The God Who Says Sorry was conceived in 2009 at one of the regular meetings a group of friends has held for over forty years. I am hugely indebted for their encouragement and advice, to Bishop Tony Foottit, Alex Wedderspoon, Dean Emeritus of Guildford, and the late Robin Morrell, Priest and former Royal Navy fighter pilot, who sadly died earlier this year.

To them must be added Hugh Bain, Canon Wilfrid Browning and Christopher Nankivell for approving and monitoring the work in its early stages, Judith Wedderspoon for her support and helpful observations, John Christophers and Claire Heffernan for their enthusiastic interest. My thanks are due to The Reverend Professor Leslie Houlden for generously scrutinizing the text and saving me from a number of errors. Neither he nor any of the aforesaid are responsible for the work's limitations. Andrea Hill has combined helpful advice and much supportive patience with her secretarial and photographic skills, contributing the images "Creation" and "New Life". I am most grateful to her, to Karen Stafford for her photo "Hope of Humanity" and to Mark Hill for his painting "Saint Mark". I am indebted to R. Piper & Co Verlag, Munich for use of the Ernst Barlach image "Die gemarterte Menschheit" 1919.

I pay tribute to Graham Cook of Writersworld Limited for publishing, to Brian Stanton for editing and to Charles Leveroni for cover designing the book: their help and advice have been a constant reassurance and I thank them.

Royalties generated from the sale of this book
will be donated equally to
Amnesty International and Barnardo's.

FOREWORD

Anthony Bird is one of the best kept secrets of the Church of England. An honours graduate in classics ("greats") and theology from the University of Oxford, he was ordained in 1958. After service as a parish priest he was Vice Principal of Cuddesdon College, Oxford until leaving to qualify as a doctor in the medical school of the University of Birmingham. After four years in medical practice he returned to clergy training as Principal of Queen's College, Birmingham.

With his abilities, qualifications and experience he seemed well on the way to a bishop's palace but chose to spend most of his working life as a G.P. in a multicultural area of the back streets of Birmingham. This book is not the theology of the library and the cloister, but one wrought out of the experience of a priest doctor who struggled daily with the joy, sadness, pain, anxiety and injustice of human life. In this profound and moving work he expounds an essential aspect of the nature of God and of the Christian faith, which the Christian tradition has shamefully neglected.

Read this book if you seek a powerful deepening of your faith. The author is a priest and doctor of great ability and dedication, respected and beloved by all who are privileged to know him.

Alex Wedderspoon
Dean Emeritus of Guildford

CONTENTS

PART 1

Creation

PART 1

Pain of the Innocent.
God's Responsibility.

"If suffering is part of the plan, the plan doesn't seem a good one to me." Some such words were spoken by Professor Hugh Pennington, eminent microbiologist, referring to his abandonment of the Christian religion (BBC Radio 4, Desert Island Discs, 17th July 2009). 'The Son of Man must suffer many things and be killed', words of Jesus (Mark 8:31). An obstacle to Christianity, insuperable to many, is the suffering inflicted by horrendous evil on innocent victims. Such suffering, often unrelenting, on a vast scale and of unimaginable cruelty is perceived to negate any assertion that God is good or that God exists. This book proposes a rational and theologically appropriate answer to what is widely seen as an insoluble contradiction, the coexistence of intolerable pain and a good Creator: it does not aim to challenge atheism for which, by definition, this contradiction does not arise.

Evil exists as a force, which typically corrupts and destroys goodness, beauty and truth. It takes life wantonly and deals in cruelty, ugliness and lies. Though a philosophical analysis of the concept of evil is unnecessary for present purposes, it is worth disposing from the outset of

1

the notion of a 'personal devil'. From a theological standpoint such a notion is a contradiction in terms: since it is characteristic of evil to depersonalize and dehumanize, it cannot itself possess the creative attributes which constitute personality, essential to its flourishing. In Mark's gospel Satan appears as pseudo-person representing both active opposition to the Holy Spirit and malign onslaught on the goodness of God. (Mark 1:12-13, 3:22, 28-29).

A menu of evil is easily compiled: war; earthquakes and other natural catastrophes; malaria; poisoning of the planet; torture; Baby 'P', and the widespread abuse of children; greed and the humiliation of the poor by the rich; Huntingdon's disease; genocide and mass murder, such as the elimination of millions by Stalin, well chronicled by Orlando Figes in his book 'The Whisperers'. Add to this the pain and torture inflicted on animals by humans: whale harpooning, dog fighting, bear bating; these are but examples of the gratuitous cruelty dealt out to animal species.

Faced with the incomprehensible scale of such evil and the suffering it inflicts on the vulnerable and innocent, monotheistic Christianity proclaims belief in God, maker of all things in heaven and earth, visible and invisible; 'All things were made by him [the Word of God]; and without him was not anything made that was made'. (John 1:3). Sole and ultimate responsibility for the whole creation is assigned to God by the prophet Isaiah in uncompromising language: 'I am the Lord and there is none else, there is no God beside me...that they may know from the rising of the sun, and from the west, that there is none beside me. I am the Lord, and there is none else. I form the light, and create darkness; I make peace and create evil; I the Lord do all these things'. (Isaiah 45:5-7, King James version)[1]. Isaiah locates evil firmly within the creative purpose of God and so assigns to God ultimate responsibility for it.

God is ultimately responsible. What does this mean? The concept of responsibility is a matter of complexity for many areas of knowledge and investigation, for example in philosophy, neurophysiological research, the social sciences and ethics. It is beyond the scope of this book to engage with these nor is it necessary: most people live their lives on the assumption that humans are, albeit within limits, responsible, and recognize responsibility when they see it. If a house is set on fire by someone with matches, a toddler or an Alzheimer patient will not be held responsible (or only to a limited extent), whereas a healthy adult may well be charged with criminal arson. In broad terms we understand what we mean by responsibility. However, some clarification of the usage made here is called for.

1. Responsibility has two senses: causative and

---

[1] 'I create evil'. It is regrettable that this translation of the Hebrew is avoided in some modern versions, e.g. 'I make peace and create evil' becomes in The Revised English Bible 'author alike of wellbeing and woe'. It is noteworthy that the Septuagint, the Greek version of the Old Testament, familiar to the early church and commonly quoted by New Testament writers, similarly translates the Hebrew of Isaiah 45:7 with its 'ktizōn kaka', meaning 'creating evil'.

curative/caring.

(a) Causative
A person is described as responsible for something/someone he/she has caused to exist (e.g. a child) or to happen (a situation or outcome). Obligation to what is created sometimes attaches to this sense, as does praise or blame. This is the meaning of responsibility in 'God is responsible for evil' and implied in 'I create evil'.

(b) Curative/Caring
This sense of responsibility connotes care, leadership, control: 'The head teacher is responsible for school behaviour'.

2. Responsibility considered as response-ability.

   Whether this connotation is justified etymologically is uncertain but is important and fruitful as it implies relationship, actual or potential, to/for what one has created or cares for. Responsibility entails the capacity or ability to respond, to relate to one's environment. Further, the notion of responsibility carries a moral sense of obligation: parents *ought* to care for their children: parenthood implies as much. Responsibility then is a defining attribute of human nature, part of what is meant by being made in the image of God (Genesis 1:27). God is responsible to and for all creation including evil: human responsibility denotes responsiveness to the world and to God as Creator.

3. Attributing ultimate responsibility to God does not negate human responsibility but contains it.

An analogy will clarify this: parents hand over to their children a degree of responsibility in adolescence, essential if they are to mature and learn from mistakes, yet the parents retain ultimate responsibility for their offspring, providing home, education and financial support.

Isaiah's proclamation of God's absolute sovereignty over creation and responsibility for creating evil (Is 45:5-7), is followed by a poem celebrating God's righteousness and its abundance 'Rain righteousness you heavens, let the skies above pour it down' (45:8). The poem concludes 'I, the Lord, have created this'. Righteousness, like evil, is God's creation. Isaiah then poses four questions:

1) Will the pot contend with the potter?

2) Will the clay ask the potter what he is making?

3) Will the child say to his father, 'what are you begetting?'

4) Will you instruct me in my handiwork?

The assumed answers are negative, but anyone familiar with Old Testament accounts of the slaughter of Egypt's firstborn (Exodus 12:29) and the whole tribe of the Amalekites (1 Samuel 15:2-

3) on God's orders, and the more recent obscenities of the Somme and Auschwitz, may demur when it comes to celebrating the Creator's righteousness.

The following incident can sharpen our focus. Some years ago a patient described how his childhood was spent in a family blighted by alcoholism and parental violence of which he was a victim for many years. The poverty was such that he sometimes went to church and school barefoot. Religious instruction every Friday consisted of a visit to the church and followed a regular pattern. The parish priest would deliver his talk to the children with reference to the large rood, with its figure of the crucified Christ, hanging above the sanctuary. Pointing to the cross he impressed upon the children that the suffering they saw there was caused by their wickedness and they could expect the fires of hell unless they repented. The priest would berate the boy in front of the class for attending church barefoot. At school he was routinely bullied and beaten by his teacher who, unsurprisingly, was a devotee of the priest. It was in middle age that this innocent victim of evil sought psychotherapeutic help for the wounds inflicted by this travesty of the cross.

What can be said, if anything, about the responsibility of God in a situation like this? What meaning does the cross have, what message for the victims of such appalling abuse? This book contends that an appropriate, albeit paradoxical, answer is available and finds support in Mark's gospel, to which we now turn.

Its evidence will be scrutinized in some detail. In a final section people's personal experiences will be considered in relation to the answer being proposed.

PART 2

Recompense and Rescue.
The Jesus of Mark's Gospel.

The crucifixion of Jesus is the centre of gravity in Mark's gospel. In this section those themes will be examined which are of special significance for an understanding of the crucifixion as God's response to evil and the suffering it inflicts on the innocent. These themes are:

The Early Ministry of Jesus

- The Response of Jesus to the will of God (1:1)
- Jesus' Baptism by John as Penitent of God's people (1:1-11)
- Proclamation of God's Kingdom: the demand for Metanoia (1:14-15)
- Healing of the paralytic (2:1-12)
- Evil
- The Poor

The Passion Narrative
Jesus' understanding of his death

- Caesarea Philippi and the Transfiguration. 'Must' (8:27-9:8)

- Jesus' understanding of his death: (10:45) and The Last Supper (14:22-28)
- The Trial (14:61-62)
- Apology
- The Centurion (15:33-39)
- Provenance
- Galilee (16:1-8)

The Response of Jesus to the will of God

Mark announces his theme in the first verse of the gospel, 'Beginning of the gospel of Jesus Christ, son of God'. This identification of Jesus as Son of God serves as title to the whole work. It is repeated, with variations, in relation to key events: Jesus' Baptism (1:11), Transfiguration (9:7), his trial before the high Priest (14:61-62), and at the moment of death in words spoken by a gentile centurion (15:39). These great proclamations give the gospel a framework and, like navigational waypoints relied on by a sailor, determine vital stages in the progress of Jesus' responsiveness to the divine purpose and his learning the meaning of sonship. They culminate powerfully in the garden of Gethsemane where at the climactic moment before his arrest Jesus, praying for relief from the inevitable agony awaiting him, finally offers himself to the Father, 'not what I will, but what you will' (14:36). Crucifixion will fulfil and complete God's work. This is the theme of the fourth gospel also: 'My intent is to do the will of him that sent me and to finish his work' (John 4:34). The words 'It is finished' spoken by Jesus at the moment of his death (John 19:30) signals crucifixion as the climax of his response to God's will. But how are we to understand this response? Mark's gospel offers a distinct answer to this question.

Martyrdom of Humanity

Jesus' Baptism by John as Penitent of God's people

John appears in the desert preaching a baptism of repentance for the forgiveness of sins. Huge crowds flock to the baptism. John heralds the advent of one stronger than himself, one whose sandals he is unfit to loose. He, John, baptizes in water, but this other (the Messiah prophesied by Isaiah and Malachi) will confer baptism in the Holy Spirit.

That Jesus is without sin is implied by Mark's account, but virtually explicit in Matthew's version of events. Jesus presents himself to John for baptism, at which John protests 'Do you come to me? It is I who need to be baptized by you'. He is overruled by Jesus: 'Allow it, for it is appropriate (for me to be baptized) to complete the whole of righteousness'. (Matt 3:13-17). Jesus is baptized and is at that moment given a vision of God and hears his sonship affirmed: 'Thou art my beloved son in whom I am well pleased', and confirmed by the gift of the Spirit. (Mark 1:10-11).

What is it that this heavenly proclamation signifies? For what does Jesus receive authentication of his sonship at his baptism? His was not a baptism on his own account for he was sinless[2], but it was nonetheless a baptism into

---

[2] 'sinless'. This is not explicit in Mark, but implied in 1:7, John Baptist's 'one mightier than I...the latchet of whose shoes I am

repentance, metanoia, for the remission of sins (Mk1:4). As such it made complete and total God's righteousness, a righteousness needing for its completion the appropriate penitence (Matthew 3:13-15). Thus, in submitting to John's baptism, Jesus presented himself as the Penitent of God's people for the forgiveness of God's people. The evangelist will have seen this event as fulfilment of Isaiah's prophecy 'by his knowledge shall my righteous servant justify many; for he shall bear their iniquities'. (Is 52:13–53:12).

---

not worthy to stoop down and unloose', and especially in 1:8 where Jesus is affirmed by John as the agent of the Holy Spirit. Jesus' sinlessness is all but stated in Matthew 3:14-15 and emphasized by the Epistle to the Hebrews (7:26) and 2 Corinthians 5:21.

Proclamation of God's Kingdom: the demand for Metanoia

After John had been arrested, Jesus came from Galilee proclaiming the gospel of God: 'The time has arrived; the Kingdom of God is near' (1:14-15). The early chapters of the gospel are a commentary on 'The Kingdom of God is near' - miracles, teachings, Jesus keeping low company, friction with the religious authorities - all are advance demonstrations of an impending revelation of divine sovereignty.

The second half of Jesus' message, 'Repent and believe the gospel', is important for our exploration and particular attention must be given to 'repent'. 'Repent' is a questionable translation of the Greek Metanoeite in the context of its occurrence in Jesus' proclamation 'Repent, and believe the gospel'. (1:15). This contrasts with its previous occurrence in John's call to baptism where the context requires the translation 'repentance'. (1:4). An accurate translation of 1:15 is 'change your mind to one of believing'; 'change your mindset'; repentance is not implied here[3].

Other reasons for rejecting the translation 'repent' in 1:15, but for retaining 'repentance' in 1:4 are these:

---

[3] On this crucial point the author consulted an eminent classicist who confirmed that in this context, as distinct from that of 1:4, repentance is not implied.

a)   The root meaning of metanoein (verb) in classical Greek is to change one's mind or purpose, in short to change one's outlook, one's mindset.

b)   Metanoia (noun) is demanded by John 'for the forgiveness of sins'. Here the change of outlook demanded has forgiveness as its objective, forcefully expressed in the Greek as 'metanoia with a view to remission of sins'. Because here the purpose of change is the particular one of forgiveness, the change required is repentance: repentance therefore is the meaning of metanoia here. (1:4).

c)   John preached repentance for forgiveness. Jesus submitted himself to that metanoia, that repentance, as Penitent for God's people, and this representative act was clearly revealed to him by God to be the acceptable and obedient expression of his sonship. In him Israel's sin was confessed and forgiven, dealt with so to speak; now the way was cleared for the incomparably stronger (than John's) message: change to trust in the gospel.

d)   In this gospel Jesus has little to say about sin and nothing about repentance. The record of his ministry in Galilee has no instance of Jesus calling for repentance and no significant mention of sin(s) after its crucial occurrence in the episode of the healing of the paralytic with its fourfold use of the phrase 'forgiveness of sin'.

These perhaps surprising features of Jesus' ministry are inconsistent with translations of

Jesus' proclamation of his gospel (1:15) giving prominence to a call for repentance which, were it correct, might be expected to herald an emphasis on repentance altogether missing in Mark's account of Jesus' teaching and preaching[4].

(e) 'Change your outlook by believing in the gospel'. For victims of suffering and evil, trust in God, the trustworthiness of God encountered in Jesus, supersedes any prior demand for repentance (and is the essential metanoia). The implications of the matter discussed in this section emerge in the episode to be considered next, the healing of the paralytic.

---

[4] The preaching of repentance is attributed to the twelve disciples sent out by Jesus on a healing mission (6:12) though Jesus' commission to them does not include 'repentance' (6:7). In this case the translation 'repentance' itself begs the question discussed earlier.

Hope of Humanity

Healing of the paralytic

Read in isolation, as for example in liturgy, this episode easily escapes notice as a deeply significant one when viewed in the wider context of the gospel (Mark 2:1-12).

(a)   Impact on the crowd. Paradox.

Before this incident Jesus' teaching and healing had already drawn crowds. His fame spread far and wide through Galilee (1:28). 'They were all amazed...what is this? A new kind of teaching! He speaks with authority' (1:27). Crowds were in attendance at the house where Jesus was and to which the paralytic invalid was carried. After the miracle the impact on the onlookers was huge: 'Never before have we seen anything like this' (2:12). Luke, reporting this incident, summarizes: 'We have seen paradoxical things today'. (5:26).

Paradoxical: contrary to expectation is the root sense of this Greek word. The impact of Jesus' early ministry was utterly at odds with ordinary expectation and experience. Paradox becomes a defining characteristic of the Kingdom (sovereignty) of God. "I say to you, stand up, take your bed, and go home." And he got up, and at once took his bed and went out...' (2:11-12). In this weak translation by The Revised English Bible, the authoritative command of Jesus to the paralytic loses much of the force of Mark's writing. More faithful to the original Greek is the Authorized Version: 'I say unto thee, Arise, and take up thy bed, and go thy way into thine house. And immediately he arose, took up the bed and went forth...' The point here is the repetition of 'Arise...arose', reflecting the significance of the Greek word (Egeiro), which later in the gospel denotes resurrection. Thus, this episode, prefiguring the resurrection, enacts the authority of God to engender trust and restore crippled humanity.

(b)   Faith (2:5)

'Jesus seeing their faith said...'

Jesus saw the roof torn apart and the invalid lowered into his presence by the carers. This, their enterprise, <u>was</u> their faith: nothing spoken, and significantly, no word of penitence. Pure faith: nothing more, nothing less.

(c)   'Your sins are forgiven' (2:5)

The inference here is that the invalid brought with him, or was brought by, guilt. To what extent if at all the organic and the psychological were combined in the paralysis we cannot know, but the evangelist presents the man as sinful and needing forgiveness (Jesus forgives him). But there is no call for penitence; Jesus pronounces forgiveness, responding not to repentance but directly to the faith of the invalid and his carers: indeed nowhere in this gospel does Jesus (unlike John) call for repentance[5]. Precision is needed

---

[5] 3:29 'everlasting sin' is a special case, discussed later. 4:12 quotes Isaiah 6:10. Mark 6:12 refers to the preaching mission of the disciples, and as in 1:15 means primarily 'change your mindset'.

here. 'I did not come to call the righteous but sinners' accurately translates the Greek of 2:17. The King James Bible (Authorized Version) has 'I did not come to call the righteous, but sinners <u>to repentance</u>': its addition of 'to repentance' is unwarranted. The presence of this phrase in the equivalent passages of Luke 5:32 and Matthew 9:13 throws into relief its absence in Mark.

Similar variations are in evidence in the texts relating to the Last Supper and have an important bearing on Mark's theology of the crucifixion. 'This is my blood of the covenant shed for many', Mark 14:24, becomes in Matthew, 26:28, 'This is my blood of the covenant shed for many <u>for the forgiveness of sins</u>', the version familiar to many owing to its usage in the 1662 Prayerbook's Prayer of Consecration. Forgiveness of sin is not, for Mark, central to Jesus' understanding of his death.

(d)   Hostility (2:6-7)

'Your sins are forgiven'. With this Jesus stirred up a hornets' nest of scribes, the guardians of religious orthodoxy. They accused him of transgressing God's prerogative to forgive. Soon after, the Pharisees, offended by the healing on the Sabbath of someone with a deformed hand, plotted his death (3:6).

It must be doubted whether the accusation that Jesus had appropriated to himself the sole authority of God to forgive takes us to the heart of the hostility and opposition of the religious. The Old Testament is replete with declarations of

God's forgiveness, for example Jeremiah (31:34), Isaiah (33:24), the Psalmist (103:3, 130:8); moreover the Law of Moses prescribed the whole apparatus and process of atonement for sin (Leviticus 4:20,26 and elsewhere).

Enter John the Baptist also proclaiming divine forgiveness. A prophetic figure, Elijah-like, heralded by Isaiah (Is 40:3; Mk1:2) and Malachi (3:1), he bestrides the opening of the gospel with his preaching of repentance for the remission of sins but also his forecast of the Lord's advent and the baptism in the Holy Spirit he will confer (1:8). Mark dates the start of Jesus' ministry to 'after the arrest of John', no accidental connection given the scarcity of chronological indications in the gospel, the inference being that John's time had served its prophetic purpose and now gave way to the occasion of Jesus' arrival.

The contrast between the two was glaring. In due course Jesus was challenged to account for his disciples' neglect of the fasting practices observed by John's disciples and the Pharisees. In reply Jesus brushes aside the charge of religious laxity, depicting the time (his time) as worthy of celebration with new wine (2:18-22).

This scenario provided the religious authority with its convenient point of attack. It was not that Jesus' words 'thy sins be forgiven thee' were of themselves blasphemous, there were precedents for this; his blasphemy consisted in pronouncing forgiveness with no requirement for contrition or penitence. In this matter John had observed the rules with his call to repentance

(1:4): Jesus had not.

John was popular, the scourge of tyranny, imprisoned for denouncing Herod's immorality, a prophet in the old mould. The religious leaders acknowledged this: disturbingly weird, he had at least followed the rulebook when it came to forgiveness. Conspicuously, in forgiving and healing the paralytic, Jesus had ignored it and flouted the Law of Moses at its core: access to God's presence lay open, available to anyone who, through change of heart and outlook on life, trusted that presence as welcoming, healing and compassionate. Scribes and Pharisees saw their authority as guardians and gatekeepers of access to that holy presence demeaned: this Jesus must go (3:6).

Evil

The scant attention given to sin in Mark's account of Jesus' ministry has been considered. It was argued that sinners, not sin, were Jesus' concern, and that taking Matthew's evidence into account, Jesus in his baptism figures as the sinless Penitent on behalf of God's people, the Righteous Servant in whom the forgiveness of Israel is assured and sin done away with as Isaiah prophesied (Is 52:13–53:12). This means that, for the Jesus of Mark's gospel, sin is dealt with, consigned to the back burner: now evil is centre stage requiring a far 'mightier' (1:7) dispensation and revelation of divine activity to counter it.

In Mark, evil is essentially the thwarter of the divine purpose and opponent of the Holy Spirit at work in the sonship of Jesus. Its modus operandi is twofold: challenge to the trustworthiness of God and the ultimate lie.

The first of these strategies occurs early in the gospel (1:12-13). The Spirit who descended on Jesus in baptism confirming him as the Son of God then propels him into the desert, there to be tempted by Satan. Even if we lacked the temptation stories of Matthew and Luke, the Marcan account, closely associating the baptism and wilderness episodes, shows that Jesus is being tempted into an infidelity to his sonship. The temptation stories of the other two evangelists demonstrate the essence of the

Satanic attack: (to paraphrase) "If thou be the son of God, then do x, y, z to procure for yourself a blueprint or guarantee to ensure the trustworthiness of God in calling you so uniquely". The poison here is in the 'if', posing as it does toxic doubt in the trustworthiness of God: 'Is it reasonable that I should go on without special assistance from God?' Evil's 'if' is countered by Jesus' assertion that God is trustworthy: 'Thou shalt worship the Lord thy God, and him only shalt thou serve'. The question is not whether, but how divine sonship is to be practised under conditions of non-divinity.

Evil's ultimate lie is manifest in the hostility of a deputation of religious leaders from Jerusalem and their accusations that Jesus owed his power over demons to evil itself (Beelzebub), thus defining the power of God (the Holy Spirit) as evil (3:22-29). This representation of good as evil and divine power as Satanic constitutes unforgivable blasphemy (whereas, by contrast, 'all sins shall be forgiven unto the sons of men'). When Jesus says to the scribes 'How can Satan cast out Satan?...No man can enter into a strong man's house', reference is being made to a traditional belief that the binding of Satan marks the beginning of the Messianic age. The inference is that Jesus is God's Messianic agent in the overthrow of evil.

Satanic opposition to Jesus' ministry is a recurrent theme of the early chapters with numerous references to the healing of those possessed by unclean spirits[6]. Peter is castigated for harbouring Satanic notions when he objects to Jesus' declaration that his Messianic destiny must be fulfilled in crucifixion and resurrection. This is the 'must' of a supreme act of faith in a loving Father's purpose for his Son, as the Transfiguration was to confirm. The suffering, trial and death of Jesus will be evil's terminal assault.

---

[6] Mark 1:23   1:27   1:32-4   1:39   3:11   3:15   3:22   5:1-19   6:7   7:25, 29-30

The Poor

The Poor

Soon after the paralytic's healing we hear of Jesus' meal with low company (2:15-17). His unconcern with sin has been discussed, but with sinners his concern is obvious, the word 'sinners' occurring four times in this meal episode. Yet sinners as such are neither preached to or about. The Nazareth sermon in Luke's gospel makes 'the poor' its focus, not sinners. 'The Spirit of the Lord is upon me because he has anointed me to preach the gospel to the poor' (Lk 4:18). Quoting Isaiah (61:1) Jesus continues: 'to proclaim release to the prisoners and recovery of sight for the blind; to let the broken victims go free'. This sermon was good news for all, sinners included, who in various ways fell short or foul of human dignity – the poor, those in a bad way.

'To preach the gospel to the poor'. The Greek word for the 'poor' literally means those who 'crouch' or 'cringe' physically, denoting beggars with their typical bent–down posture. 'The poor' serves as a general term for those afflicted in any way, especially those who have to beg to maintain life. 'The poor', those cringing in spirit, morale, or physical dissolution, are much in evidence in the Old Testament with which in its Greek translation the Septuagint Mark was familiar. 'He lifts the weak out of the dust and raises the poor from the rubbish heap' (Ps 113:6); 'I know that the Lord will give to the needy their rights, and justice to the downtrodden (Ps 140:12); Hannah's song (1 Samuel 2:8) echoed by

Mary, mother of Jesus, in the Magnificat praises God for exalting 'them of low degree' (Lk1:52); God 'giveth right to the poor' (Job 36:6).

It is to the poor then that the Righteousness of God is directed. This is a constant theme: 'With Righteousness shall he judge the poor' (Is 11:4). 'I, the Lord, speak Righteousness' (Is 45:19). In the early ministry of Jesus the Old Testament vision of God's Righteousness towards the poor is realised. The healing of the paralytic dramatically enacts the Psalmist's: 'He lifts the poor out of the dust'; crouching beggars are accorded their proper stature and dignity. The compassion of Jesus for the hungry multitudes is stressed in both stories of their feeding (Mk 6:34, 8:2), signalling the universal reach of God's purpose for the poor.

Caesarea Philippi and the Transfiguration. 'Must'.

This section (8:27-9:8) is the pivot of the gospel and its midpoint. With Jesus' arrival in the Caesarea Philippi region the mood and content change. Hitherto his preaching and healing ministry has been, by and large, public, constantly raising questions about his identity (1:27, 2:6-7, 3:11, 6:2-3, 8:27) extending even to the natural world, 'Who is this that even the wind and sea obey him?' (4:41).

From now on the miracles are fewer and the public aspect of Jesus' work, though not absent, gives way to private instruction to the close circle of disciples particularly on the necessity and proximity of death and resurrection. This fearful destiny is prophesied three times (8:31, 9:31, 10:33) and dominates the narrative of Jesus' journey south to Jerusalem to fulfil this destiny. 'He began to teach them that the Son of Man must suffer many things and be rejected of the elders and of the chief priests, and scribes, and be killed and after three days rise again' (8:31). This crucial passage itself pivots on the single word 'must', the sense of which pervades also the two later prophecies (9:31, 10:33).

Peter, who had first confessed his recognition of Jesus as the expected Messiah, is outraged by Jesus' identification of his Messiahship with a necessary destiny of appalling suffering. Peter's protestations are countered by the savage accusation of Jesus that he harbours Satanic designs against obedience to the divine will. Peter was not alone in his confusion: after the second prophecy 'the disciples did not understand what he said, and were afraid to ask' (9:32).

'Must' is prominent elsewhere in the gospels. The boy Jesus who delayed his departure from the Passover festival in Jerusalem told his anxious parents that he 'must be about his Father's business' (Luke 2:49). The two disciples walking to Emmaus on Easter Day, confused by the events of Good Friday and the reports of the resurrection, are overtaken by the unrecognized Jesus who chides them for their obtuseness: 'Must not the Christ have suffered to enter his glory?' (Lk 24:26). 'Must' is implicit in Jesus' insistence on baptism by John 'for thus it becometh us to fulfil all righteousness' (Matthew 3:15).

Jesus' unwavering insistence that his Messiahship must entail crucifixion as the fulfilment of his obedience to the Father's will is decisively confirmed by the Transfiguration. Mark links the Transfiguration episode to the Caesarea Philippi prophecies by the chronological indication that it was 'after six days' Jesus took Peter, James and John to the mountain (9:2). There the same heavenly voice heard by Jesus at his Baptism now declares, but this time to the disciples, that 'this is my beloved Son' and 'hear him', him, that is, who had come to understand that sonship now entailed, now required of him the destiny of crucifixion and resurrection. This was to be his response to the Father who loved him, a response to fulfil the Father's purpose for his creation.

The gospel's threefold emphasis on the 'mustness' of the crucifixion raises the question: what had to be achieved by crucifixion, which could not otherwise have been achieved? It takes us to the fundamental question of this book: what revelation of God's righteousness not merely proclaims concern for the poor (innocent victims of horrendous evil) so frequently expressed in the Old Testament, but actually embodies and effects divine responsibility for them decisively and completely? These questions lead on to the Passion Narrative of Mark's gospel (chapters 14-16).

Jesus' understanding of his death

(a)   Recompense (Deliverance)[7]

The Son of Man came not to be ministered unto, but to minister and to give his life a recompense (lutron) for many (10:45).

The traditional translation of the Greek lutron as 'ransom' has caused havoc in theology and incomprehension for many Christians. Ransom, the price paid to secure release from captivity, to whom is it being paid? Who is requiring it? 'Ransom' is not the inevitable translation, usual though it is. Lutron has two other, closely associated meanings, recompense and deliverance, so that the phrase in question is better rendered 'to give his life a recompense for the sake of many'. Jesus, then, presents his coming death as recompense for the sake of many, the many being those to whom the recompense of deliverance is due, the victims of evil.

(b)   The New Covenant

'This is my blood of the new covenant poured out

---

[7] The translation of lutron as recompense is recognized by Liddell and Scott's lexicon, but the authority for it in classical Greek is slight. Lutron and its cognates mean deliverance and are commonplace in the Septuagint. The notion of deliverance as recompense, antapodosis, has Old Testament support. Isaiah (ch. 35) foretells God's deliverance of Israel and speaks of it as recompense (verses 4 with 10).

for the sake of many', spoken by Jesus at the Last Supper (14:24).

The additional phrase 'for the remission of sin' produces 'this is my blood...poured out for the sake of many for the remission of sin', a version familiarized by Matthew's gospel and the Prayer of Consecration in the Book of Common Prayer. It is not present in Mark, and is absent in Luke (22:17) and Paul (1 Corinthians 11:25).

This observation is not pedantic. Mark's version supports the contention that the forgiveness of sin is not of primary concern in his understanding of the death of Jesus, (the same point previously demonstrated in connection with 2:17).

'For the sake of many': the phrase occurs both here and in the passage just discussed (10:45)[8]. Here the context is Jesus' presence with his disciples for the Passover meal commemorating the deliverance of the Jews from oppression in Egypt. The covenant now declared by Jesus is for the many, not for the disciples exclusively: Jesus had enjoyed eating with the poor and being with them (2:16). The Last Supper inaugurates a new covenant whose meaning and purpose is to be founded on and proclaimed by his death and its gift of deliverance and recompense to victims of evil.

---

[8] The Greek prepositions are different: Anti (10:45), Hyper (14:24); each can mean 'on behalf of', 'for the sake of'.

(c)   The Sword of God (14:27)

As the narrative moves from the Last Supper to Gethsemane Jesus tells his disciples they will all be ensnared, quoting Zechariah's prophecy (Zech. 13:7) 'I will strike the shepherd, and the sheep will be scattered', an abbreviated version of the complete sentence, 'Sword, awake against my shepherd, and against him who works with me, strike the shepherd and the sheep will be scattered and I shall turn my hand against the lambs'. The message is uncompromising. The approaching horror and death of Jesus is the responsibility of God; the disciples are powerless to obstruct the onslaught. Some brave soul wielded his sword to chop an ear off one of the temple police but it was an irrelevance: 'The scripture is to be fulfilled' Jesus says, his death being divinely purposed (14:49). The sword of God is poised to smite, even at the professed loyalties of his followers.

The Trial

The high priest questioned Jesus, 'Are you the Messiah, the Son of the Blessed One?' 'I am', Jesus replied 'and you will see the Son of Man seated at the right hand of the Almighty and coming in the clouds of heaven' (14:61-62). These are the last words of Jesus before his final cry of dereliction (except for his brief answer to Pilate), spoken as the hostility of the authorities climaxes in his arrest, trial and death sentence. This confession of his identity is distinctive:

- It is spoken by Jesus himself (in contrast to the Baptism and Transfiguration proclamations of the Father) in answer to the question 'Are you the son of the Blessed?', the title 'Blessed' being used because God's name was too holy to be spoken. Jesus replies 'I AM', this divine name constituting a full face challenge to the lies and corrupt power of the High Priest and his entourage whose accusations masquerade as true religion. This is God confronting evil.

- It prophesies the subjugation of evil by the Son of Man who represents God's ultimate sovereignty, authority over and responsibility for evil.

- It is a solid affirmation of trust in the trustworthiness of God, trust that his present ordeal is required of him by a loving Father. The inner conflict in accepting his Father's will as his own had occurred just hours before in Gethsemane (14:36).

Previous proclamations of Jesus' identity as Son of God had provided divine authentication and the progressive revelation of the meaning and demands of this identity.

- Jesus' identity as son of God revealed him, in submitting to John's baptism, as Penitent of God's people, and commissioned him to take the gospel to the poor.

- Jesus' identity as son of God at Caesarea and the Mount of Transfiguration entailed the 'must' of crucifixion and resurrection as recompense to the victims of evil.

- Jesus' identity as Son of God at the Last Supper and in Gethsemane inaugurated a new covenant and committed him to sharing torture and death with victims of evil.

This learning and living out divine sonship under conditions of non-divinity was sustained by a constant metanoia, the persistent exercise of response to and trust in the Father's will amid the unfolding of events. Confronted by bogus accusations and certain death, Jesus' faith bursts into a visionary identification of himself as Son of Man, God's agent in the coming Kingdom of Righteousness with its demolition of evil and restoration of creation's glory.

(Mark 14:63-64)
Found guilty, Jesus is condemned to torture and death. As a trial this was a charade: his accusers with their plotting and perjury were guilty of violating innocence in the name of godliness. Yet it had to be: such was the plan and will of God, the divine must of crucifixion. So by what conceivable mechanism of morality or device of faith can this be represented as the doing of a compassionate Creator? Where in the whole drama is any ingredient of divine love to be found? The glaring contradiction between the facts of innocent suffering and faith in a compassionate deity finds its resolution not in the theoretical formulations of theology, though these have their uses as indicators, but in the crucified person of Jesus who embodies the contradiction in himself, bringing to bear on it a love which reaches the hellholes of pain. Embodying both the victim of evil and the Creator responsible for evil, Jesus speaks from the cross becoming the Word of God's apology, the I AM who says sorry.

Auschwitz-Birkenau: Unfathomably Shocking

Apology

There appears to be no biblical instance of God saying sorry. To what extent does the gospel of Mark support this concept? Examination of the evidence suggests that an interpretation of the cross as divine apology, while not explicit, is compelling.

To recognize that repentance for the forgiveness of sin is not at the heart of Mark's theology clears the way for a better grasp of what the gospel does say. Its main focus is not on sin but on evil, and in two respects. First, the destruction of evil. This is central to Jesus' ministry, a sign of the coming Kingdom of God, the Messianic binding of Satan and the liberation of God's people, notably the poor, 'those who have it bad', the innocent victims of evil. Secondly, the power of evil (Satan) manifests itself in attempting to thwart the sonship of Jesus, the learning and practice of which requires total trust in the trustworthiness of God the Father.

The word 'must' is the pivot of Mark's theology in the gospel's central section (Caesarea Philippi and Transfiguration) where its threefold reiteration forces acknowledgment that the suffering of Jesus and the evil it represents was willed by God. This accords with the weighty insistence of Isaiah's prophecy (discussed in Part 1) on God the Creator's responsibility for evil. Yet the cross, with its suffering and death, is God's chosen instrument for the annihilation of evil, and brings back the question made unavoidable by the 'mustness' of this gospel: what must the suffering and death of Jesus have achieved which nothing but his suffering and death would or could have achieved?

Pointers to the answer are forthcoming in Old Testament declarations of God's righteousness and justice, not least in the Psalms and the prophetic writings:

- (Psalm 140:12)
  'I know that the Lord will give to the needy their rights and justice to...the downtrodden'[9].

- (Isaiah 61:1)
  'The spirit of the Lord is upon me because the Lord has anointed me...to announce good news to the humble, to bind up the broken-hearted,...to proclaim liberty to the captives, release to those in prison'...the passage quoted by Jesus in his inaugural sermon in Nazareth (Luke 4:18).

These passages foretell the deliverance of the innocent victims of evil and the recompense owed to them by divine justice for their suffering. Recompense is how Jesus spoke of his death at the Last Supper; so what precisely is the nature of that recompense, the deliverance that could be conferred by no other means than by the suffering and death of Jesus?

---

[9] Revised English Bible translation.

We are treading holy ground here. Referring to Auschwitz, Rabbi Irving Greenberg has said: 'No statement, theological or otherwise, should be made that would not be credible in the presence of burning children'. The only statement a serious visitor to Auschwitz might find credible, and the only one with any claim to integrity, is unique: the confession of apology. But in that hell the apology has credibility only when spoken by one ultimately responsible for the horror, and integrity only when spoken from the place of agony where alone that plea of apology, the 'I am sorry', can be heard by those to whom it is due.

Recompense, apology, saying 'sorry' is the necessary and essential mode of God's righteousness, the 'must' of crucifixion, first because it is owed to the poor, the innocent victims of evil in every epoch and as such is an expression of God's nature as righteous; and secondly because it acknowledges divine responsibility for evil.

Apology is not a formula, and the mere formulation 'God says sorry' does not constitute an apology. The very notion of an apology for Auschwitz, or any other such hell, debases the meaning and currency of the word and minimizes the unfathomable scale of the suffering and evil involved unless the essential criteria of genuine apology are satisfied beyond compromise.

Real apology has clear hallmarks:

- It acknowledges responsibility

- It recognizes that recompense is owed to victims

- It restores honour and dignity

- It requires humility

These criteria are satisfied in the crucifixion, having been foreshadowed in the ministry of Jesus:

- The 'must' of the cross in the purpose of God, asserting His responsibility

- The suffering of the cross is recognition and measure of the recompense owed

- Honour and dignity are restored by Jesus' identification of himself with the dehumanized

- 'They clothed him with purple, and platted a crown of thorns, and put it about his head' (15:17)

The meaning of the cross as apology is paradoxical inasmuch as it manifests Jesus, who, in his baptism by John, appears as the penitent of God's people bearing their sin to God for forgiveness, now in the baptism of his death (Mark 10:38) is manifested as the penitent of God embodying His apology to creation and its victims of evil. In John's baptism Jesus was revealed offering the penitence owed by the people to God; now in his suffering and death he is revealed as the penitence owed by God to His innocent poor.

The paradox here is mirrored in other paradoxical expressions of Christ's work and nature in the New Testament:

- Jesus washing his disciples' feet
  (John 13:4-5)

- Jesus 'being in the form of God...took upon him the form of a servant'
  (Philippians 2:7)

- 'The foolishness of God is wiser than men and the weakness of God is stronger than men'
  (1 Corinthians 1:25)

- God made Christ to be sin for us, who knew no sin; that we might be made the righteousness of God in him
  (2 Corinthians 5:21)

It could be argued that any and every understanding of the cross must, to get anywhere near the truth, be paradoxical to the point of near incomprehension, passing all understanding. There is precedent: those first encountering Jesus, Luke reports, 'were all amazed, and they glorified God, and were filled with fear, saying, 'We have seen paradoxical things today'.

It is apparent then that the elements which characterize sincere apology are woven into Mark's presentation of Jesus' ministry and passion. There is however another hallmark of the true apology if it is to carry conviction. It must entail change of heart and attitude, metanoia, and guarantee future change for the better, in particular a new and creative responsiveness in any relationship involved. This forward-looking aspect of apology informs the last chapter of the gospel.

The Centurion

'When the sixth hour was come, there was darkness over the whole land until the ninth hour. And at the ninth hour Jesus cried with a loud voice...My God, my God, why hast thou forsaken me?...And Jesus cried with a loud voice, and gave up the ghost. And the veil of the temple was rent in twain from the top to the bottom. And when the centurion, which stood over against him, saw that he so cried out, and gave up the ghost, he said, Truly this man was the Son of God'.

The irony and paradox pervading the Passion Narrative extends to this last of the 'Son of God' proclamations, voiced by a centurion, infidel, alien, agent of Roman imperial brutality. From Caiaphas and the temple of God, lies and cruelty; truth from an officer in the army which would destroy it within forty years. The centurion's declaration is in direct response to the manner of Jesus' death and his cry of dereliction 'My God, My God, why hast thou forsaken me?'

- 'My God, My God'. Jesus appeals directly to God his Father. Like his agonized prayer in the Garden of Gethsemane it is an appeal of profound and immediate trust.

- 'Why hast thou forsaken me? Not 'why have I been abandoned?' (passive tense) but 'why hast <u>thou</u>...?' God is responsible for the abandonment.

God's Apology

- The essence of evil in this gospel has been its attempt to subvert the Son's trust in the Father, insinuating the untrustworthiness of God. Through the centurion the evangelist witnesses to a faith ('My God, My God') unflinching in attributing to the Father responsibility for abandoning His Son Jesus to torture and death as a criminal. Against such trust in the divine purpose, evil has no purchase and meets its own annihilation.

'The curtain of the temple was torn in two from top to bottom'. (15:38). Entry into The Holy of Holies through the veil or curtain shielding this innermost sanctuary was forbidden on pain of death, except only to the high priest on the Day of Atonement, then and there to make expiation for himself, his household and the whole assembly of Israel (Leviticus 16:1-2). Instantaneous with Christ's death is the rending of the veil. Yearly the veil was entered by the priest passing inwards, bearing the penitence of the people to God's presence. Now by act of God the veil is torn from within as God passes outward to offer in Jesus His penitence to the suffering.

'If that nation, against whom I have pronounced, turn from their evil, I will repent of the evil that I thought to do unto them' (Jeremiah 18:8). Jeremiah prophesied God's change of mind and outlook towards a contrite people: now from the cross God repents of the evil done to the innocent poor.

The centurion, unlike the women watching from a distance, was not to witness the resurrection. Yet in his words 'Truly this man was Son of God' there may be detected the recognition that 'this man's death and the manner of it' as well as his own role as executioner pointed, contrary to all expectation, to the reality of the God whose Son this was.

Provenance

It is worth considering the gospel's provenance at this point. Mark may have written it in Rome. He was there, for a time at least, with Paul (Colossians 4:10, Philemon 24) and a reliable tradition records his deriving information about Jesus directly from Peter.

Both Peter and Paul were martyred, probably in 64 A.D. during the emperor Nero's persecution of the Christian community in Rome. Mark himself is believed to have been martyred in Alexandria about 68 A.D. Reliable facts about the gospel's date and authorship are hard to establish. What is certain is that its author wrote in circumstances of danger and brutal persecution of Christians, supported if not instigated by Nero, as the contemporary historian Tacitus records. The possible relevance of this provenance will be considered later.

Saint Mark

Galilee

There is no resurrection appearance of Jesus in this gospel, but the news 'He is risen' and the promise to his disciples at the Last Supper that after his resurrection he would lead them into Galilee is announced by the youth at the empty tomb, with the assurance 'there you will see him as he told you' (16:7).

'There you will see him as he told you'. The morass of uncertainty about this ending of the gospel makes speculation a risky business but we are surely on safe ground in asserting that seeing Jesus in Galilee amounted to more than a mere sighting, a sort of forensic identity parade to confirm, along with evidence of crucifixion, the recent reports of resurrection as reliable. The point of the meeting, predicted by Jesus on the night of his betrayal, would be the recognition and revelation of what was incomprehensible before the resurrection event. Passing through Galilee on his way to Jerusalem Jesus had taught his disciples the necessity of his death and resurrection, 'but they did not understand what he said and were afraid to ask' (9:32). Now he was to lead them to see, recognize and comprehend the meaning of his obscene crucifixion and the news 'He is risen' which had so stupefied the women at the tomb (16:8). Their dutiful errand gave them a shock, which drove them bewildered, speechless and scared from the scene. The summons to see not the body they came to embalm but a resurrected Christ in Galilee required of them and the disciples a reversal of purpose, a metanoia more profound than any previously demanded. It took them back to the proclamation they heard at first: 'The Kingdom of God is near; respond and trust in the Gospel'. Their eyes opened in meeting the risen Christ, they appropriated, made their own that first Galilean proclamation, themselves identified as bearers of God's recompense and apology to the victims of evil.

Galilee is where it all began. Jesus came to John's baptism from Galilean Nazareth. Capernaum, the Sea of Tiberias, the homes and jobs of the disciples were there, and from there Jesus had uprooted them with his demand for metanoia, the reorientation of their understanding and outlook to one of trust in his message of God's sovereignty.

Viewed from Jerusalem, Galilee was an alien sort of place: 'Galilee of the gentiles' (Isaiah 9:1) whose folk spoke a different dialect (Matthew 26:73). The beneficiaries of Jesus' healing work there had been 'sinners' (Mk 2:17), 'unclean' characters like lepers and the demon – possessed (1:23,27,40), those of low repute (2:15), the vulnerable and innocent such as children (9:36-7). These were 'the poor' of Jesus' Nazareth sermon (Luke 4:18), the cringers, the bowed down victims of evil, (Greek for 'the poor' literally means those who crouch and cringe). When Jesus defined his death both as recompense and new covenant 'on behalf of many' (10:45, 14:24) he meant these poor.

So it is to Galilee, the place of the poor, that Jesus will return to be recognized as he gives to the poor the apology owed to them by God. An apology, it was noted earlier, to be complete entails change of heart and attitude, the metanoia which guarantees a changed future for the relationships involved. Hence the promise of seeing the Risen Jesus validates God's 'sorry' from the cross, guaranteeing evil's overthrow and the healing of creation and humanity.

Galilee is where the original proclamation of the gospel is to be re-enacted and communicated, and the disciples recommissioned to speak the word of God's apology. It will not primarily be a call to repentance. Slaves, battered children, the underclasses, sellers of the Big Issue, tortured prisoners, asylum seekers, folk without a voice, sick and dying, the depressed with their secret hurt and loneliness, these all have guilt enough heaped on them by society, by states, by churches. For them Jesus' New Covenant is gift without admission charge.

The disciples were called back to Galilee. The New Testament and birth of the early church testify to the first apostles having derived authority for their mission from their encounter with the Risen Jesus. Yet no such encounter is described by Mark, in contrast to the other three evangelists. Their Resurrection appearances are no 'happily ever after stories' but episodes integral to the particular and distinctive portrayal of Jesus characterizing each gospel. They carry through and complete, each in its own way, the understanding and meaning of Jesus presented in their narratives up to and especially in the crucifixion. The endings of Matthew, Luke and John are not interchangeable.

Mark's omission therefore need not be regarded as any sort of loss or deficiency but rather as an essential component of this gospel's dynamic. In this sense his last chapter will complete that understanding of the cross which is particular to his gospel, as is the case with the other three. Mark's silence about the encounter of the Risen Jesus with his disciples carries a message of its own and is remarkable considering his certain knowledge that the event took place, and that through Peter he had direct access to the momentous experience of that occasion.

Mention of Peter is apposite here. Surely an apology was owing to him and to the other disciples. Their frailties, desertions and denials, so far from establishing their responsibility for Jesus' death, threw into sharp relief the relentless and inevitable unfolding of divine purpose; God's responsibility is always to the fore in Mark's account. It is scarcely conceivable that Jesus did not say sorry to the friends he had led to the gates of hell and then bade follow him to Galilee. Yet Mark refrains from describing any meeting despite his awareness of the profound, indeed unique significance of the event in question.

Instead we have the stupefaction of the women who came to the tomb. The ending of the gospel is powerful and dramatic: 'They went out quickly, and fled from the sepulchre; for they trembled and were amazed: neither said they anything to any man, for they were afraid'. As well they might be, for they were on holy ground, close to Golgotha. Theirs was the primaeval awe of the holy. Moses experienced that awe when he met

God in the flames of the burning bush and heard the voice, 'Put off thy shoes from off thy feet, for the place whereon thou standest is holy ground (Exodus 3:5).

'Jesus said sorry to his disciples'. These words are not of themselves an apology. No report of an apology such as this, nor a description of an apology, is an apology. Apology, the 'I am sorry', consists in its being communicated, experienced. This experience of receiving Christ's apology, foundational for the church and its mission to the poor, with its shock and amazement, awe and wonder, tears and joy, the incomprehensible union of a compassionate penitence with the glory of the Creator of all things: to this experience of the first apostles on meeting the Risen Jesus Mark brings, through omission and silence, the recognition that he treads ground too holy for description.

It must be remembered that closer in time to Mark than the death and resurrection of Jesus were contemporary events centred in the Colosseum of Rome. There, Christians were perishing in hope of reunion with Christ after martyrdom: 'There you will see him'. For them, we may justifiably imagine, Galilee symbolised this hope and the recompense guaranteed them by the cross. Peter after all was present, at least until Nero caught up with him, to remind them just how uncompromisingly Jesus had insisted on the must of crucifixion and resurrection.

New Life

PART 3

The Power of Compassionate Apology.

Recompense for injury done is a requirement of moral law and natural justice. A doctor, whether by accident or through negligence, causes the death of a patient. Litigation ensues, financial compensation offered and the doctor is admonished or otherwise punished by his professional body. Even so, the dead person's relatives are aggrieved: 'If only the doctor or hospital would apologise'; 'why won't they just say sorry?' The deceased and, by association, friends and relatives have been dishonoured. It takes an apology to rectify this and restore honour. No price can be put on honour.

Patients with a history of abuse and emotional deprivation can be helped in psychotherapy to rid themselves of crippling guilt and the sense of worthlessness inflicted by childhood trauma and thereby discover their innocence. (Exploration into innocence is not a bad description of psychotherapy). Their birthright of dignity, honour, confidence, love previously denied them is in some measure restored. I have sometimes asked patients in the course of their psychotherapy 'Do you feel you are owed anything?' Their answers were similar: 'Acknowledgment'; 'being visible'; 'a hearing'; 'an apology'; 'getting rid of shame'; 'dignity'. A priest has told me of a 'shock' he experienced in the course of his therapy with a highly regarded analyst. She had let him know that she was a non-practising Roman Catholic and, in a particularly painful session, told him that she could readily receive communion from him at Mass. Asked for an explanation, her startling reply was along these lines: 'I can identify with the pain you feel. Taking communion from you would acknowledge that, and be offering the apology due to you in a way I think you would recognize'.

Recompense is the necessary manifestation of God's righteousness owed to the poor, the innocent victims of evil in every epoch. The nature and character of that recompense was radically new and paradoxical. Predicted and foreshadowed in those features of Mark's gospel discussed above, Jesus' death and its meaning revealed a shocking truth: Jesus' identification of himself with the poor, and his identification of himself as fulfiller of the Father's will showed him (and eventually his disciples) that his crucifixion, and only his crucifixion, could complete his Messianic vocation to bind Satanic evil and restore their humanity to the poor.

The final acceptance of that destiny in Gethsemane signalled the fruition of a life characterized by constant renewal and deepening of metanoia, the transfiguration of understanding, purpose and vision which was the learning and the meaning of sonship: God the Father was righteous and willed the annihilation of evil and the recompense of its victims. In Gethsemane Jesus saw and accepted that his death was purposed by God ('not my will but thine be done') and as such must be, and was meant to be the revelation of his righteousness: a demonstration that Golgotha, the heart of darkness and evil, anti-God, anti-human, anti-creation, was the occasion in history when the power of evil is cancelled.

To say that God overcame evil on the cross is a commonplace teaching of Christianity, an essential truth, but imprecise and worn too smooth by bland repetition. As I write, news comes of the Pakistan floods with their thousands dead and millions homeless. Recently we heard of a woman who set fire to herself and her daughter, victims of relentless bullying by local children. The word from the cross to those so tormented cannot be 'your sin is responsible', nor even 'you are forgiven'. The language of repentance and forgiveness utterly fails to meet the case, to right the wrong. It cannot be otherwise than that the Jesus who knew himself named by God in his baptism as Penitent for his people's sin came, in the baptism of his crucifixion, to know himself as Penitent for God, speaking God's 'sorry' to the innocent victims of creation for the evil for which, ultimately, He as Creator, is responsible.

The scope of the Creator's response to (responsibility for) evil extends beyond humanity. Malaria, locusts, earthquakes, hurricanes, drought exemplify evils of natural origin and cosmic scope conventionally termed, and not without irony, 'acts of God'. Such phenomena cannot be excluded or excused from divine accountability without fatal damage to the coherence of Christianity or other monotheistic faiths. If we are to speak of God's apology as Creator to His whole creation, it becomes the task of monotheistic apologetics and the would-be appropriateness of mission to develop sensitive languages and idioms of apology.

One proposal for such an apology is offered by Beth Crisp in her recent article 'Beyond Crucifixion, Remaining Christian after Sexual Abuse'[10]. Referring to the Australian Aborigines and their culture she shows the way in which society comes to recognize the hurt and harm it has inflicted on an oppressed, racially different people and traduced their deeply held traditions and culture. Crisp's concern is to provide appropriate formulas and rituals of apology whereby children abused and violated by the churches and clergy can be apologised to. Repair and restoration of the dignity of the oppressed is at stake here. The approach advocated by Crisp in her excellent article with its challenge to churches to acknowledge their responsibility for abuse mirrors the large-scale enactments of apology and reconciliation on the national and international stage, apologies for the slave trade, apartheid in South Africa, genocide in Rwanda

---

[10] Beth R. Crisp. 'Beyond Crucifixion, Remaining Christian after Sexual Abuse'. Journal of Theology and Sexuality. Vol. 15 No. 1 2009.

being recent examples.

The development of sensitive languages, idioms and models of apology are required if God's 'sorry' and the deliverance it offers to creation, the environment and humanity is to be heard and received. For the poor, the innocent victims of evil, the gospel which is presented as a call to repentance for the forgiveness of sin is either incomprehensible or demeaning. It is only where the poor are, where God is, that the still small voice of His 'sorry' can be heard, and its compassionate language learnt and spoken.

The explorations of this book have been concerned solely with the question of the compatibility of God's righteousness and the co-existence of evil[11]. Earlier in this book evil was characterized as a force which typically corrupts and destroys goodness, beauty and truth, takes life wantonly and deals in cruelty, ugliness and lies: essentially it is anti-personal. Conversely,

---

[11] 'Does God exist?' has not been our question: we have not been concerned with arguments for God's existence. On the other hand, the question 'What sort of God do we believe in?' neatly labels our theological sphere of operation. It has yielded the response that, given the existence of evil and the suffering of the innocent and poor, this is the sort of God we must, of theological necessity, believe in. Even atheists have their gods.

Lurking in wait is that fundamental mystery: 'why does God create evil?' as Isaiah insisted to be the case if God is to be God. This problem is not avoided here because of its apparent insolubility, for searching into mysteries may reveal a rich harvest of insights, but because its investigation is not essential to an understanding of Christ as God's response to evil and its victims.

any manifestation of beauty, truth, generosity, nurture of life and personality whether communal or individual, presents faith with scope for recognition of the Creator at work. Divine apology is a necessary and essential part of the process whereby evil and the suffering it entails are embodied on the cross and come to be recognized as the Creator's responsibility and integral to His purpose, the truth and reality of which are validated in the encounter and experience of the Spirit of Jesus crucified and risen.

"Martyrdom of Humanity", the sculpture of Ernst Barlach (died 1938): the image of which appears earlier in this book, serves to illustrate what may be termed the power of compassionate apology, Barlach's own commentary on his work being "I must be capable of compassion", "Ich muss mitleiden koennen". The power of the image derives from its creator's engagement with, indeed his identification with his creation. Its power consists in his compassion, the "suffering with" that his work had to absorb to conform with the prescription he set himself. It becomes appropriate to probe this compassion deeper since this term, like love, is vulnerable to devaluation through random or glib usage. What then is the character, the particular stamp of compassion Barlach chiselled into that piece of oak? Generosity, forgiveness, help and self-sacrifice are modes of compassion but the martyred figure cries out for none of these; it is surely the compassion of apology that Barlach requires his own creation to require of him and the beholder. What energizes the relationship of tortured figure with creator or beholder and breathes life into this hanging wreck of humanity is the power of the compassionate apology its silence demands.

The New Testament warrants differences in viewpoint and interpretation of the significance and meaning of Jesus' life, death and resurrection for humanity and the cosmos. This book emphasizes an interpretation appropriate to the plight of innocent victims of evil, one demanding attention to the reality and power of divine apology, to the God who says sorry to His creation.

SOLI DEO GLORIA